Caged-In Little Girl

My Path to Deliverance and Healing

Carrie Thomas

Published in 2019
Printed in USA by KDP/Amazon
www.kdp.amazon.com

Table of Contents

Acknowledgement

To That Special Someone (You Know Who You Are)
I thank God that you can hear and be obedient to His voice when He speaks. He sent me one of His angels of mercy who delivered a message of grace and compassion. We serve an awesome God who calls Himself Our Father . . . as well as our friend. The scriptures He spoke to you on my behalf stayed on my heart the rest of the day.

This morning (April 21, 2007), early in the a.m. (3:00 – 4:00), a light, soothing breath of wind blew upon me. I lay in my bed for some time, God's Word racing through my mind. Finally, I arose, got my Bible, went to my prayer room and sat still on the floor, awaiting His instructions.

I opened my Bible and went to Numbers 6:24-26, then to Psalms 23, 51, 91, 121 and finally, to Ephesians 6. These scriptures were already highlighted, indicating this place was familiar. God helped me to tie up my Bible (meaning I read every referenced scripture for each verse). The Lord heard my cries and responded. I cried and He comforted me. A peace and refreshing of the Holy Spirit came upon me.

Glory to God! Because of your obedience, I have been renewed, strengthened, and restored. And, for that, I pray blessings upon you that God will continue to manifest the desire of your heart. I pray one hundred-fold returned blessings upon you, in Jesus Name. Amen!

His Servant!
My Sister-in-Christ!

Foreword

Two cannot walk together unless they agree. This is what the author of this manual has done; agreed with the word and the voice of God in obedience for the mandate HE has called her to carry out. This book will bring hope for a courageous journey throughout your life's circumstances. Carrie has learned to put God first and trust Him no matter what life brings; and she knows, with the help of the Lord, you will come out successful and victorious. Can true love exist and forgiveness be imputed to those who make life difficult, when you find yourself placed in an unhealthy environment?

Well, this book reveals God's triumphant grace for a changed, hopeful, abundant, courageous, and happy life. As Carrie's heart was filled with a determination and persistence for a new beginning, this book reveals her loyalty to God who changes lives, because LIFE MATTERS TO GOD. What a blessing to know you have a purpose in life, and that you can live a life of abundance, health, prosperity, and success when you let God come in and take control. This magnificent and powerful author, evangelist, and prophet, Carrie Thomas, has written this book to be a blessing in your life.

—Donetta Best, Chief Apostle, Truth of the Living God Prophetic Ministry

I have had the pleasure of knowing Carrie Thomas for several years. During those years, I have known her to be a woman of faith, integrity, and consistency in her walk with God.

Carrie has proven to have a heart for others. She has started an Outreach Program that touches the hearts of so many lives and brings hope to many hurting people. She is truly exemplifying the heart of God.

Carrie is also a powerful intercessor in the Kingdom. In addition, I have seen many examples of her ministry and talents. And, I have been impressed by her Christian character and diligence to fulfill her assignment on Earth.

I congratulate her ability to accomplish writing this book while maintaining a home, being a wife, mother, and grandmother. Her determination in reaching her goal has been admirable. Therefore, I am grateful and confident in saying Carrie has been called for such a task.

—Pastor Charita Coleman, Dream Center Church

Introduction

I was born in Denmark, South Carolina, in the cool of the night at Bamberg Hospital. One of my fondest memories as a child was the birth of my youngest sibling. When my mom gave birth to her, we were not allowed in the hospital; so, my dad lifted each one of us to the window outside of her room, so we could all have a peek at the new baby. She was the most beautiful baby girl I had ever seen. On her wrist, she wore a pink beaded bracelet with her name on it.

We all started elementary school in South Carolina before moving to the big city of Washington, D.C. in June of 1958. There were no buses to take my siblings and me (three sisters and two brothers) to school, and the walk was long.

Living in D.C. was exciting for small children coming from the country. Everything looked huge and grand. We moved into a small pink house behind my grandmother's (father's mother) apartment building. The whole family was together, and it was wonderful living with my parents and siblings. My mother stayed at home and took care of us in the beginning. Later, there was a need for a second income, so my mom started working.

We had a live-in babysitter who my parents knew from Denmark, South Carolina. I'm going to call her Ms. Tee. She was very nice and we didn't want for anything. My dad would do the shopping and the pantry would be full of treats, but we were not allowed to eat them without asking first. My mom was a wonderful cook and I wish I had more of her recipes, but she seldom wrote her recipes down (I later learned her penmanship and spelling were at a third- grade level). My mom did not finish elementary school, so it was a challenge for her to spell certain words. Her gift was cooking, and she did it well. When it was dinner time, my youngest brother could not wait until my mom called the family for supper. He would take a slice of cornbread or a biscuit and find a hiding place under the bed to eat it. But he always got caught. My mom would take the handle of a broom and shove it under the bed until my brother came out of his hiding place.

Together, we would laugh until tears rolled down our faces. Our early years as a family were the happiest of my life.

When you think about it, family is a precious gift created by God. The first two chapters of the book of Genesis talk about how God created man from the ground, stood back, and observed His own work—then gave Himself accolades because He thought His handiwork was very good. But, then, He said man needed a helper, so He created woman by using a rib from man.

Another joyful family memory was the time my father brought home our first color television. At least that's what we thought he was carrying when he walked through the door holding a big bulky object. He plugged the television into the socket, turned it on, and covered the screen with a color sheet. To my siblings and I, the picture appeared to be in color. One thing I've learned is how little it takes to please a child. We screamed and hollered the whole time we watched that black and white television. My father was an awesome dad who took care of his children.

Summer Vacation in the Country (Denmark, S.C.)

After the school year ended and vacation started, our things were packed, and we were sent to the country to stay the entire summer with our grandparents in South Carolina (my mom's father and mother). My youngest sister had been sent to live with our grandparents when my parents separated, so we looked forward to our visits because we got to see our sister.

My grandmother was short in stature and small framed, but she was a strong, black woman of the South. I later learned she did missionary work in the neighborhood. I recall attending the little white steeple church, and after the service, the women would go to their cars and retrieve food that was prepared for Sunday evening fellowship.

My grandfather was six feet tall with a bulky frame. He worked on the mill and during a few summer afternoons, I was tasked with taking him his lunch. At exactly twelve noon, the lunch whistle would blow and I would start my journey across the field. In one hand, I carried the brown sack holding his sandwiches and in the other hand, his jar of sugar water. My granddaddy loved his sugar water.

One summer, we went to visit and my granddaddy was bedridden. It was as though time had fast-forwarded because I didn't remember him being sick. Grandma was his caretaker and she refused to let anyone else tend to him. She would feed and wash him like a newborn baby. Using white sheets to cover him when he needed to be changed, my grandmother would change and wash him. We played outside and when the pain was unbearable for my granddaddy, I would hear him screaming at the top of his lungs, "Doll, hand mercy on me," and she would say to him, "Thomas, what is wrong with you? Stop all of that hollering."

After my granddaddy went to be with the Lord, my grandmother never had another man in her house. We continued to visit every summer and then, there was a long break. Later, when I had a family of my own, I continued the tradition and took my children and husband to grandma's house for summer vacation. My childhood years were memorial because I got to spend precious times with my grandparents. It left an impression on my heart and today, I have the same spirit about my grandchildren. They can come and stay with me anytime they want and, as matter of fact, my daughter tells me she needs to deprogram my youngest grandson when he comes home from visiting, because we let him have his way so much.

As children, my siblings and I were taught to pick cotton. Around five o'clock every morning (except for Saturday and Sunday), we were awakened and dressed to go with Mr. Henry (a white man) who came in his black pickup truck to pick us up along with other children from the neighborhood.

This was a time I did not care for, but there wasn't anything I could do about it. From sun-up to sun-down, we dragged those sacks through rows of white, fluffy cotton bulbs until they were all picked. At the end of the day, those sacks would be bulging with cotton and Mr. Henry would weigh each sack (one cent for each pound).

This money helped to buy food while staying with our grandparents during the summer months. On the weekends, each of us were given a quarter to spend as we wished. Of course, we all wanted to go to the movies in the city. As black children, we were never allowed to use the front entrance, but rather, the side entrance with a lot of stairs to climb and only one way in and one way out.

Some of you may be wondering why I'm writing this book. As a woman, I've carried the hardships, tragedies, and terrifying times from childhood that were buried deep in my subconscious because they were too hurtful, or I just didn't want to remember them. I believe my total deliverance and healing will come to pass from writing this book.

Chapter 1

The Life of a Child in a
Dysfunctional Family

The temperature in the room seemed to rise as I felt Dad's shadow spread over us. It was Sunday morning and I was sitting while Mom combed my hair. By the tone of his voice, I sensed he was angry and bent on arguing. Mom obliged him and as the confrontation escalated, I became so frightened that I couldn't move. Keeping my head bowed and not wanting to look up into that darkness, I suddenly felt the warmth of moisture covering my body. The sweat on my forehead and upper lip beaded to a glisten. My eyes welled up but I did not cry. Trickling down my spine, the trail of moisture seeped into my underwear, causing my disturbed bladder to betray my imitation of calm. I began to weep...and seep. Small pools of water collected everywhere. Then, there was the blood. As it dripped down my eyelids and through my lashes, I thought it was my own. But then I realized it was Mom's.

Irritated by her audacity to exchange words, Dad pulled out a switchblade and slashed her across her breast. She tried to shield me by pushing me away, but I had already leapt from between her legs and ran full-speed out the back door. Bounding to jump over the full flight, I thought I'd never get to the bottom of those four stairs and into the yard. I lost my footing two steps in and landed in a patch of dirt and bramble. On the ground, my wet body created a lumpy paste of mud and pebbles. Now, it's my own blood I feel.

Still lying on the ground, I notice my left knee had landed on a piece of glass protruding from the unkempt flower bed. Hurting both physically and emotionally, tears finally poured down my face. I heard screams and commotion filtering down to the first floor as my mother struggled to defend herself. My parents were up those stairs fighting and cursing one another, while being completely oblivious to me lying on the ground and hurt. No one came to my aid. No one was concerned about my cries.

My parents were totally absorbed in their argument. My siblings, hearing the escalating voices, had already battened down in secret places of safety we all had created in small, remote spaces of that little pink house. We scurried to our various foxholes to escape the reality that any one of us could be next to experience the consequences of being in the wrong place at the wrong time. There were no assigned spaces. Whoever got there first staked their claim. Someone would squeeze behind boxes under the bed. Another would lie in the bathtub behind the double-hung shower curtains.

Being outside now, my bunker would be a crawlspace to the left and behind the stairs. I scrambled there and pulled my frame into the same fetal position my siblings would be hiding in. We all would wait for quietness. As a ray of sun crept through a space in the framing of the stair, I examined my scraped knee. In my distress, I was still more concerned about who would take care of my mother's injuries. I wanted to take the risk of going back to help her, but I was the child.

My mom was wounded. "Who will help her?" I wondered. My instinct, even as her little girl, was to protect her. And, I wanted her to protect me. So, that day, I created a new, secret place for myself. I called it a Dream space. There were no first-come, first claim in this hiding place. It would be all mine — still dark and out of view. It's there that I would begin to suppress the rage and helplessness I felt when my parents fought.

In that space, I stood over my parents. I demanded and commanded the fighting to stop. I made them love each other – and me. There would be kisses and hugs for all of us. It's a small and massive place, all mind and mine, and everyone would be there with me. In this space, I could keep the secrets of my reality and what I really felt. If they were real, I could hide them. I could even determine if they were dreams and hide them, too. Did this really happen? No, it couldn't have because it was something painful. I would not allow pain in this place. There would be no flinching, no crouching, and no folding into fetal positions in this hiding place.

My parents separated when I was nine years old. Moving to New York City after the separation, I rarely saw my father for several years. He passed, before my mom, of cancer. But I remember when he would visit, he always gave my children a new five-dollar bill. One Saturday, my dad was visiting with me and I noticed the back of his shirt was bloody. I asked about it and he said it was nothing. My dad was in excruciating pain, but he did not believe in doctors. I don't remember my dad ever being sick a day in his life, and he never had a check-up until his illness.

We were all called to the hospital before he died. I stood in the hallway because I wanted to remember him as the funny and loving dad, he was to me as a child. His favorite treat for us was root beer floats (vanilla ice cream and root beer soda). My husband went into the hospital room and stayed with my dad until the end, while I stood on the other side of the door crying my heart out.

Chapter 2

Little Pink House - On the Corner

Looking out of my bedroom window with my siblings, we watch as our mother leaves us unattended after our father has left for his night job. Crying and wailing, we shout out, "Mommy, don't leave us. Stay home," but she doesn't acknowledge us. We leave from the window and settle down in our own beds to sleep. We have a live-in babysitter who is a close friend of our parents, so we're not entirely alone.

In the early hours of morning I'm awakened by a noise. It's my father returning home from his night job. He goes from room to room checking on us and realizes mom is not in the house. I go back to the window in my room looking for the car that took mother away last night and suddenly it appears.

But I realize I'm not alone. My father is standing with me at the window. My mother unlocks the door and comes upstairs where my father is waiting. They begin to argue and next there are blows as they move towards the bathroom, where my mom falls into the bathtub. She's bleeding and bruises cover her body. Then, the telephone rings. It's bad news. Aunt Ada is calling to say her youngest son, Jay, has drowned while swimming.

Things seemed to settle down after that horrible night. It was a rule in our house that we had to take naps and one day, while asleep on the living room sofa, I was startled out of my sleep by the touch of someone else on the sofa with me. I turned to see my father's brother who is attempting to fondle me. I scream and someone (it's unclear who) comes to my rescue. The incident is shared with my father who later confronts my uncle. There is a terrible fight and their brotherly relationship is broken. My father bars my uncle from his life and our home. I escaped this horrible attempt at incest, but one of my siblings didn't. Later, as adults, my sibling shared this horrible experience with me. We are all keeping dark secrets.

Everyone needs a go-to person. Someone they trust enough to confide in and tell all their darkest secrets. It's the start of any healing process. My mother and father were separated, and so were my siblings and I. We were scattered across the country. Some of us were sent to live with our grandparents, some with great aunts, some with mom, and another remained with dad. This was the breakdown: my oldest sister stayed with my mother (local area), I went to stay with my father's mother (local area), my brothers went to stay with my father (New York City), and my babysitter went to stay with my mother's parents (Denmark, S.C.).

Years later, my mother gathered all of us back together. But, by then, we were like strangers to each other because communication and visitation was so irregular. As sisters and brothers, we had to get acquainted all over again. It took years for us to feel comfortable around each other. It was as though we had to build a new love and trust. Today, we are still wounded from this ordeal. I'm the second oldest between my oldest sister and the sister right below me. We have no sister to sister relationship. Someone is always competing for the other's attention and affection.

My relationship with God has also placed a wedge between us. So, my oldest sister and the one right beneath me have a closer relationship. But, when one gets angry with the other, they call me. How do you deal with one of your sibling's telling you that the other one does not like you? It's not easy but, for the sake of peace, I continue to be a mediator and pray that one day God will completely heal us.

If you have children or plan to have children, please be sure you're ready. You will be responsible for those children for the rest of your life. A broken home will damage children in ways we can never comprehend. I know this because the curse has repeated itself throughout my life and the lives of my siblings. We all had children out of wedlock and no longer have relationships with their fathers. And, I refused to allow my children's father anywhere near them until the day he died.

I took my children to their father's funeral. Of course, they knew who their dad was, but a father-child relationship was never established. I pray to this day that I haven't damaged my children the way I was damaged by my parents. Both of my parents are dead now, but their legacy lives on through us — good or bad. However, I do not want to continue this generational curse, passing it on to my children and grandchildren.

The curse stops here. I have confessed my sins, gone through deliverance, and rededicated my life to God. He is the only one who can save us from this corrupt world. If there is any hardness of hearts in the family, we must come together and forgive one another. I'm not just writing a book; this is a letter of how my life went through fire and water and how I survived. The only way this was possible was nothing more than fulfilling the purpose God predestined for me before I was placed in my mother's womb - Jeremiah 1:5, NKJV. He foreknew me and chose my parents' DNA; but the life I lived then and now was God's plan for using me for such a task as this.

So many people kept telling me, "There is a book on the inside of you that must be written." Ten years ago, I would have never put on paper what I have written. But at this point in time, I'm not concerned about what you think of me and how you feel about the things I write. My deepest, heartfelt concern is that someone is set free after they read through the pages of this book. Everything I have written may not apply directly to you, but indirectly; it's very likely you know somebody, somewhere, who can relate to one of these chapters.

Chapter 3

Homeless at the Age of Twelve

I was a runaway. One Sunday afternoon when I was twelve, I was home alone suffering another punishment and, once again, grounded for what I deemed a petty offense and for something which was totally out of my control. I was a bed wetter, and my bladder always told on me when I was afraid or nervous.

Even when I tried to put on a brave front, certain disturbances, especially any confrontations in which there was blood or loud arguing and cursing by my parents, might cause me to lose body fluids. I couldn't control my parents' behavior or my body's reaction to it. Mom punished me every time this occurred and this time my punishment was no picnic, literally.

Before the incident, my parents had planned a picnic and I was so excited. I had seen other families lazing on the grass, eating sandwiches, and drinking pop. They all looked so carefree, relaxed, and happy. We had never been on that type of outing. I envisioned we were going to evolve into a Norman Rockwell version of a loving family. So, I felt I was being grossly mistreated to have to miss out. Everyone else was going, but I had to stay in my room.

I became so angry that I went as far as scheming a way to get back at my mom in the most hurtful way I could. I thought that running away from home was the answer, but it turned out it wasn't. On and off, for eleven years, I lived from house to house, sometimes sleeping on the streets.

One night, I walked through a school playground and a gang of boys saw me. I was gang raped. What could be worse than being repeatedly raped and one of them contemplating ruining me for life by thrusting a bottle into my vagina; yet, it did not happen because one of them prevented this from happening. I ended up being saved from being permanently damaged. So, I was saved by a rapist and I kept it a secret.

As a runaway, I kept in touch with my siblings and found out that my oldest sister was getting married to a gangster. I went to the wedding and I will never forget that bright sunny day. I wore a purple chiffon dress. I knew I would not stay for the wedding, which was held in a house my mother was renting. The gangster was a resident in my mother's basement; and every time my mother went out of the house, she would tell him what would happen to him if she caught him messing around with any of her daughters. My sister and the gangster found a way to have a relationship anyway.

The wedding was over, and it was time for me to leave and go back to the streets. I cried, but I didn't stay at my mother's house. There were too many bad memories there. Instead, I returned to the place where I was staying and then the dreams began. Every night I would dream of falling through a black hole and never reaching the bottom. I would wake up drenched with sweat. This went on for months, until I reached a decision to move back home with my family. When I did, I was treated like the black sheep.

Many families have a black sheep or skeletons in their closet. I remember a birthday so clearly when my oldest sister gave me a present. I was so excited because no one had ever given me a gift before; however, I opened it to discover that the gift she had wrapped so nicely had been worn by her first, then rewrapped for me as a gift. I was devastated but I didn't quit. This time, I was determined to make my life work.

Dating a Black Panther

In the 1960's, there were different kinds of gang-related activities. It was more about equality, regardless of your skin color or texture of your hair. Being involved with a Black Panther, I got to see the other side of people's thoughts and charisma through the behavior of a group of people who were determined to stand together, no matter what. But there was another side that no one would ever see, if they had no relationship or entanglement with the group. Remember, the environment and the people you allow into your life determine what you will become.

I took on the mindset of these people before I realized it, and carried the residue of their behavior to my job. One day, I had a confrontation with a programmer on my job. By now, I had learned to stand on what I believed to be true and this person was trying to change my thought pattern to align with theirs. The confrontation became heated, and I was called a "spicy wench." How many of you reading this book can relate to why I felt like crushing this person with the backlash of my tongue (B.C.- Before Christ - days)? But, for some reason, another feeling came over me. I had a feeling of victory.

Another name given to me was Angela Davis (my Black Panther name). She was well-known back in the 60's and 70's. I did not realize the change that had captivated me, until I was given a different name and the workplace confrontation occurred. I needed someone to help me and not judge me. The only person who could make this happen was the God I had heard about through attending church with my grandmother, whom I lived with when my parents separated. I was in church Sunday-to-Sunday it seemed. So eventually, the relationship with the group ended, and I never again saw the Black Panther I dated for a season.

Chapter 4

A House of Gambling
Instead of a House of Prayer

Moving home took me off the streets for a minute. Living with my mom and five siblings was not an easy life. My mother sponsored gambling parties every weekend, and having strange men and women moving about the house freely was not a good thing. The sleeping arrangements for me and my sisters was in a shared bedroom with one bed. We could hear my mom and her guests gambling, drinking, and making lots of noise. One day, it finally happened that one of her guests decided to creep around, ending up in our room where I was wide awake and waiting for him with a baseball bat. We had no more problems after that night.

Exposing children (especially your girls) to strange people is an open invitation for the devil to run rampant in your home. I remember the many boyfriends my mom had after she and my dad separated. One particular boyfriend became the father of my baby sister's child. When it was known that my sister was pregnant, she wanted to give the baby up for adoption but my mom said no. She did not believe that this man would do such a thing. My baby sister went into a deep depression and never returned. She has lived most of her life as a homeless person to this day.

For the past thirty-plus years, she has lived on the streets of DC. I know that there is a God because she has survived many horrible nightmares. I can remember while I was pregnant with my last child and we were contacted by the hospital to come on behalf of my sister. My doctor advised me not to go because I was in my ninth month of pregnancy; he did not want any spontaneous reaction to what I was about to witness.

When we arrived at the hospital, the nurses and doctors prepared us for what we were about to see. My sister's head was the size of a watermelon. She had been beaten almost to death. During this incident, someone had taken the handle of a broom and rammed it into her vagina. My God, my God, I thought. You promised that You would never leave us or forsake us: Hebrews 13:5, NKJV. God, were you there when all this happened?

Humanity says girls or boys or women or men are to blame for the horrible injustices that take place in their lives. Now, you know that many rapes are not reported for many reasons. Sometimes it's shame, pride, or being blamed for something that was out of their control. This is literally a crime against the soul of an individual. Who can you share this horrible experience with: your mother, your father, your siblings, your teacher — who? And, how can you do it without feeling as if you are the reason the crime took place. Humanity needs help.

During this time in my life, I was in a dark place. I had

become a rebellious child over the years from watching, hearing, and being part of a battle that was not mine. It was hard to believe that hell existed in a different place and time because I was living in a hell on earth in my daily life — if you want to call it living. And, living as a homeless person, there are things that you will never share and will take with you to your grave.

I believe the longest time period during a person's life are the nights. This is when the demons walk the streets portrayed as things like the beautiful schematics of Washington, D.C., the capital of the world. Where is the compassion and passion for the homeless? While living like this, I attempted to go back home but was not welcomed. I tried to live with my grandmother, but it did not work. I had dropped out of school and tried to go back, but wasn't able to. I was giving up on myself because I could not get anyone to pay attention to a broken and hurting little girl. "Where is society when you need them, and where is your family when you need them?" I wondered.

We lived in a neighborhood that those who did not live there would perceive as a good neighborhood. I believe it was, but the people were not so nice. It is true that people make up the church and the same goes for any neighborhood. So, now I'm thirteen and another rape is brewing. But, this time, the people are not strangers where I am. I was visiting the home of a so-called girlfriend and had no idea that she had set me up to be gang raped by some of her male friends.

As they took turns raping me, she and her sister knew what was happening. I felt that I was always setting myself up, always in harm's way. When would this cycle of my life come to an end? The shame and disgust overwhelmed me, yet I still looked for love in the wrong places. You sometimes think the environment you're in is safe but, it can be another doorway to hell. So, be careful who you call your friends.

By now, my resentment was so big that I didn't like myself and none of my family. I felt as though no one wanted to be around me, and I felt the same way towards myself. How do you get your dignity back after years of physical and mental abuse caused by family members, friends, and strangers? This little girl was caged in, and the person holding her hostage did not want to let her out because she would remind her of the bad and haughty experiences hidden somewhere deep in her being.

The time finally came, and someone wanted to set the little girl free. Was it the one who has her caged or another? She's an adult now, and her past is keeping her from her future. The new person is saying repeatedly, "Set her free, set her free, you have to let the little girl free, so you can move into your future." I am the only one who can set her free. I have the key that will unlock the door to the cage where the little girl resides.

This story of my life is not easy to write, but my total deliverance will arrive through the words written on these pages. Let's keep on the path of resurrection and freedom for this little girl. She's caged in and only I can set her free. Has the time finally arrived for me to set her free? It's not just my life that's dependent upon her freedom, but also the lives of my children and my grandchildren. There are others waiting for me to set the little girl free. The people who are now in my life need all of me, not just a part of me. Every part of me is reserved for someone out there who has a caged-in little girl or little boy. I must set them free through freeing the caged-in little girl in me.

Chapter 5

I Think I'm A Woman

Finally, I'm off the streets and back home with my mother and siblings, yet living a promiscuous life. Drinking, drugging, partying, and sexing. At the age of twenty-two, I had no children, worked in a bar as a waitress, worked at a dry cleaner's, and spent money like there was no tomorrow. Living what I called a life. Sleeping all day in a stranger's bed and living a street life at night. By now, I'm hard-core and care about no one, not even myself. Looking for love in all the wrong places. And now, it's my day off and night is approaching, so it's time to get ready to party.

I go to a club everyone has been talking about, not knowing that this will be a turning point in my life. At this club, I met a bartender on parole whom I fell madly in love with. Later, he would become the father of my three children.

Unwittingly, I have embarked upon another hellish situation, and will live it out for the next seven years. It will involve physical and mental abuse. I'm sipping my drink and flirting with the bartender to try and get his attention.

Finally, he sees me and the romance of horror begins. As it went on, it got to a place where I wasn't allowed to see the people I used to laugh with and talk to in the bar. This man did not want anybody around me while I waited for him to get off work. One cold, winter night I went to the bar and someone spoke to me and he saw them. At the end of the night, after the bar closed and we were on our way back to my mother's apartment, he started to argue with me. The next thing I knew, he had grabbed me by the hair and knocked me to the ground.

This man literally dragged me at least 10 or 15 blocks. And, in the process, there were people passing who would not help me. This is a night that will live with me for the rest of my life. As a young woman, I thought his behavior was his way of showing me how much he loved me. So, the relationship continued, and the next thing I knew, I was pregnant with my first child. I later discovered that another one of his victims and I were pregnant at the same time.

I remember a moment during my pregnancy with my first child when life didn't have any meaning for me. And, I didn't think about the life that was growing inside me. Desperate and alone, I attempted to end the life of my unborn baby, but every attempt failed.

There was another time in my life when I entertained the thought of committing suicide. I planned how and when I would end my life. This was before the hotshot (my children's father) at the bar. I thought he was the man who would be the love of my life, but it turned out not to be so.

Looking for love in all the wrong places, I realized the relationship was not going the way I expected it to. After swallowing a bottle of pills, for the first time in my life, death was knocking at the door. But, for some strange reason, I dialed my mother's phone number. It seemed like hours had passed before I heard the knock at the door. And, when I opened it, there stood my mother with intense fear on her face.

She grabbed me, ran outside to a cab that was waiting, and rushed me to D.C. General Hospital. When I got to the emergency room, my mother checked me in and told the attending nurses and doctors what I attempted to do. All I could hear was someone saying, "Walk her," but the heaviness of sleep overpowered me. The next thing I knew, I was being rushed into a room where the pumping of my stomach began. This was one of the most horrible things I had ever experienced. My mother took me home with her and cared for me. I never went back to that place where darkness crept in and I tried to take my life.

Life is a planned and predestined journey, but without the proper guidance, it can throw you a curve. I had no mentor or example to follow for how to live a whole and complete life. People who are hurting hurt others, because it's a way to cover up their pain and turmoil. Just like Adam and Eve who, after eating of the Tree of Life, started wearing fig leaves to cover up their shame. That's what people do. We make a mess of our lives and try to blame others for what we have constructed.

Life is choice-driven, and we can frame our own world. But instead, we cover ourselves with fig leaves. We go through life wearing masks to disguise our real selves, pretending to be on top when we are at our lowest. The enemy tricked Adam and Eve into thinking there was more to life than what God was sharing. After they failed the test, they were dismissed from the Garden of Eden (Paradise). The devil didn't bother them again, because their actions gave the devil the upper hand. How many times did your mother or your father tell you not to do something and you did it anyway? That's how we open the door for the enemy to come in and run rampant in our lives. If I had a second chance, there are things I would not do. But you can't turn back the hand of time. On my job, we are always creating lessons-learned documents, so we don't repeat the same mistakes. I believe we can create a lessons-learned manual for life and pass it on to our children. If you do what mommy did, this is what can happen.

We can help our children to not make the same mistakes by sharing our life experiences. I hear people say it's bad to share one's personal business. But there is nothing we have experienced that somebody else hasn't. Yes, I can say that because God is all knowing, He's everywhere, and He's all powerful. I am a true believer that what's in the dark will surface to the light. I am a true believer that what you sow, you will reap. I sowed a lot of bad seeds in my lifetime and I am reaping the harvest now. There will always be a harvest, whether bad or good, because reaping time is coming.

Watching my children grow from babies to childhood and then adulthood, many of my bad seeds were reproduced through them. If you don't want a bad harvest, then don't sow bad seeds in the first place. Bad seeds can be planted through words you speak or through your thoughts or actions. Remember: "death and life are in the power of your tongue: and they that love it shall eat the fruit thereof" (Proverbs 18:21, NKJV).

There are generational curses we inherit from our parents and who inherited them from their parents, which have not been broken; and, there are curses we have passed on to our children. Alcoholism is a sickness and disease that has been around forever. There are alcoholics in my family now, and there were some in the past whose weaknesses have been carried on. Who will break the curse of alcoholism? Alcohol is a drug that will take a life just as quickly as cancer by causing you to develop cirrhosis of the liver.

The bus stops here. I have cursed my children with drugs, alcohol, suicide, and promiscuous living, but it stops here. I have been clean for twenty years, and my cleansing will continue because I met a man named "Jesus" and gave my life to Him. Since then, I have been living a clean, free life. I didn't have to go to AA, because I believe it's from the pit of hell. I know it's for those who say they can't control their habit, but God has given all of us free will.

You can do anything or quit anything you desire. When I went to the altar and rededicated my life to the Lord (May 1998), every desire I had that was not of God was left at the altar. The Word says, "I have given to you life and death, choose life" (Deuteronomy 30:19, NKJV). God provides you with life changing promises in the Bible (66 books).

There are things that I have done which God had said don't do; but I made my own choices and went my way instead of God's way. Life is a journey, so please choose carefully, whether you will take the "wide gate" or the "narrow path" (Matthew 7:13-14, NKJV).

Chapter 6

Shacking Up (Common-Law Wife)

Moving out of my mother's home was not a good idea, but at the time, I thought I was in love and living with the love of my life. We had moved into our own apartment; one day the phone rang and he answers it, receiving information that the other woman had lost her baby. Of course, he said it was my fault, so he took it out on me. I will never forget trying to reach out to his family. What a joke. His family thought this fool did no wrong, so I might as well have been talking to the wall.

My baby girl was born and it was the happiest time of my life. Her father had no job and the money we were receiving was from welfare. He took the welfare checks and gambled with them. The relationship went from bad to unbearable in seven years.

When I was on welfare and pregnant with my first child, I no longer had contact with my family; I lived in fear from day to day. I wasn't permitted to answer the door or go outside. I lived in a prison of my own making. Day in and day out, my activities consisted of watching soap operas and eating. When it got dark, my common-law husband came home. There is an old saying that love is blinding. I would consider this statement to be more real and true than any other I have ever heard. My blind love and fear kept me from leaving and reaching out to my family.

When I became pregnant with my second child, a boy, I was on top of the world. My children became the love I should have been receiving from the man in my life. I wanted someone to love me so bad that I can remember telling God (before I was saved) that if He would give me children, I would love them unconditionally and God answered my prayers (not knowing at the time that God had already predestined my life to have children at this specific time – His time). After the second child, we moved because we owed back rent; but this fool kept taking my welfare check and gambling with it (gambling houses, race tracks, other women, etc.). He was taking food out of my babies' mouths, and there was nothing I could do about it. I had to find a way to feed my children. Sometimes, as women, we must come to a place in our lives when we say enough is enough.

Living in Fear

One day, I took a bold step and called my oldest sister. She came with milk and Pampers, but I was afraid and refused to answer the door. My sister knew I was in the apartment and left the packages at the door. I was peeping through the blinds, and once she was out of sight, I went to the door and brought the packages into the apartment. I cried a lot that day, but refused to let anyone in. I was in a place where I knew it was time to escape my prison and venture into the world of the living; but I didn't know where to go or who would help me.

My social worker introduced me to a training program where I could receive the education to prepare me for a job in the government. When I was in school, learning was not a barrier but a challenge to do my best while growing up in a dysfunctional family. I completed the program and took the Civil Service Exam and passed. I was contacted by the Office of Personnel Management (OPM) for three different positions and chose the one that was on the bus line, making it easy for me to travel back and forth to work. When I went for the interview, there was a stipulation in the application that you would not be hired if you were pregnant.

I had just found out that I was three months pregnant with my third child. I lied about my pregnancy, because at three months I was not showing. Now, the fire is seven times hotter because of my last pregnancy and the father of my children was never home. One night, he came home from the race tracks after suffering a big loss. I was the closest target to take out his anger and frustration on, so he hit me in my pregnant stomach. I was afraid my baby would not live but she survived. God watched over me during this era of my life, and I gave birth to a beautiful baby girl.

A few months earlier, when I was attending the training program, my neighbor across from where I lived was taking care of my two children. I came home from training one day and the person caring for my children met me at the door, letting me know she ran out of milk and Pampers. So, I went up the street to the store and returned to find her acting nervous and crying. I asked her what was wrong, and what she told me was not what I wanted to hear. One of her male friends had been released from prison, and she had let him take my daughter and hers and he had not returned. I lost it. I screamed and cursed her so badly that I thought I would lose my mind. I ran to my house and called the police. They came and started to question me as if my daughter would be found dead. I fainted, and when I came to, they were waving smelling salts under my nose. The babysitter was near and I told her if anything happened to my baby, she might as well take her last breath. Just as I got the last word out of my mouth, my baby came running down the sidewalk. This was one of the happiest days of my life. The police asked me to take her in the bedroom and remove her undergarments to make sure there was no evidence of child molestation. We moved from that location to another apartment across the creek.

Single, Parenting, and Working

I was a working mother with three children and nothing had changed in my relationship with their father. One day, I was getting ready for work and my common-law husband came into the bathroom where I was combing my hair and grabs a handful of my hair. The pain was excruciating. He knocked me down beside the bathtub. My oldest child was watching. I believe the word of God where it talks about "out of the mouth of babes and suckling hast thou ordained strength because of thine enemies; that thou mightiest still the enemy and the avenger" (Psalm 8:2, NKJV).

My baby came into the bathroom, knelt beside me, and placed my head in her lap saying, "Mommy don't cry; it's going to be alright." She was two years old, and I will never forget the comfort I felt from those words and the touch of her little hands. But, for some reason, and I don't know what happened to this day, I experienced a strength and boldness that came over me and a new journey began for me and my babies.

My life began to move in a different direction, and I tried to stop the intimacy between myself and my children's father but it was a battle. I refused to participate, but it was taken without my consent (I was raped over and over). I finally reached a place in my life where enough was enough. I went downtown and filed a complaint for a civil protection order. When he found out, he went berserk. I was granted the civil protection order and as I was leaving the courthouse, he was on one side of the rail and I was on the other, I remember his words to this day. "I am going to kill you," he said. He was ordered to move out of the apartment, and he was not to come within 100 feet of me and our children. The fight for my life and the lives of my children had begun. At night, I would push the living room sofa against the front door to keep him out, but it was useless. I woke up one morning and the sofa had been removed from the door. He called me on the phone and said, "If I wanted to kill you, I could have cut your throat in your sleep last night."

There was another time where horror invited itself into my life. My baby girl was six months old and I was trying to make peace with my children's father. He came to visit and he took my baby without my permission to Baltimore, Maryland. This was a devastating time for me. I begged him to please bring her back and I don't know who convinced him to return her, but he did.

Chapter 7

The Gun at My Head

I thought my children's father was out of my life, but he wasn't. He showed up again at my mother's residence. I had taken the children over to my mom's place to spend some time with her and he knocked on the door. I had told my mother that he was not to come near me, but she shook it off because she liked him. My mother believed all I had gone through up until this time was my fault, so she let him come into the apartment. When he entered, I felt an uneasiness, but I didn't know what it was until I noticed him keeping his right hand in his pocket. Suddenly, he pulled out a gun from his pocket and placed it to my temple.

My mom screamed, "Please don't kill my daughter!" By the time he let me go and ran out of the apartment, the police were in the hallway. Someone must have heard all the screaming and called them. They arrested him, but first they examined the gun. It was a water gun with the appearance of a real gun. A person who is not familiar with guns would have thought it was real.

The scars from the relationship with him left me wounded for a long time. Because the fear was so severe, I started drinking to wash away the memories. The drinking provided a way of escape for a moment; however, when I became sober, terror was waiting. So, I went to the next level of getting rid of the memories through drug use. As a druggy, I slept during the day and roamed the streets at night. Working as a bartender, I met a lot of strange people from drug dealers to gays to gangsters. The song that says "creeps come out at night" was so very true.

I can remember, though not clearly, being in someone's apartment with a bowl of powder sitting in the middle of the coffee table with small, thin spoons all around it. I indulged until I passed out. When I woke up, I thought it was the next day — but it was three days later. This really frightened me because I had lost track of time. I had a girlfriend who worked at a topless go-go club at night. We were hanging tough and for some strange reason, I never got involved in that type of dancing. The money was nice, but I had a problem with the exposure.

I fell in love with my girlfriend's brother who already had a girlfriend. Men are greedy creatures. Instead of choosing one of us, he slept with both of us. Sometimes, she would catch me with him and sometimes I would catch her. It was crazy but, you know what, in the end, he didn't marry either one of us. He married a girl from Philadelphia. Years later, he got in touch with me to have another go at it and I met him at a club. Believe it or not, my infatuation was over and I didn't feel butterflies like I use to when I was pursuing him. It was over.

Chapter 8

Survival after the Breakup

Every day, going to work was a living hell. Walking to the bus stop, I looked around for signs of my children's father. At work, he would call me 24/7 so I couldn't work in peace. When I left work, he would be standing across the street watching me. God, I thought, when will this end?

After enduring months of sleepless nights and being terrified during the day, it suddenly stopped. I didn't want to have anything to do with men after this. The experience caused me to curse all men. My life was my children and nothing and nobody mattered until God sent me an angel one day. But, I wasn't convinced enough to start a new relationship. We started to see one another slowly. Before I knew it, I was dating and thinking my nightmare was over.

My angel and I were invited to a colleague's home to shoot pool and have some fun. It was an amazing evening. I had not felt like this in years, but was still afraid to commit to a new relationship. After the evening was over, my friend drove me back to my apartment and we said good night. At this moment in my life, it was a friendship and nothing more. It was raining, and as I was walking toward the front door of the apartment building, I could hear footsteps running in the rain behind me. I thought nothing of it and continued to walk. And then, the next few minutes felt like the end of my life.

My children's father had been waiting for me to return home. He hit me so hard, I fell and my body landed between the outside and inside of the hallway of my building. He began to bang my body with the door. I thought this would never end. He grabbed my hair and pulled it out by the roots. One of my neighbors heard the commotion and opened his apartment door, but then, closed it. I was thinking no one was going to help me. I thought about my children. Who was going to take care of them? But suddenly, my neighbor reopened his door and stood there with a sawed-off shotgun and pointed it at my children's father saying, "If you hit her again, I will blow your head off." He stopped beating me and ran. I couldn't move, so my neighbor and others helped me to my apartment.

Someone called the police and they came by. Then, I had a stroke and my face started to twist. The police wanted to take me to the hospital, but I was too scared to leave my apartment. I can't remember if I ended up going to the hospital or not, but God saved my life once again.

The police brought a bag to me that had a mass of hair. One of them went into my bedroom and saw my baby girl standing up in her crib. He picked her up and said, "Who could hurt someone as beautiful as this one?" My baby was six months old and my birthing wounds were still healing. It's almost as if I've blocked everything relating to that moment out of my mind or buried it deeply within my subconscious.

I believe God is allowing me to remember so much because it's time for me to receive my healing and deliverance in every area of my life. My prayer is that this book will be a blessing to everyone who reads it. Free the little girl (or boy) who has been caged inside you all those years. I am so free now that I want everyone who is not free to experience what I am now (free). I have shed a lot of tears during the writing of this book, but it was necessary. It's part of the cleansing and purging process of my soul.

Chapter 9

Healing after the Storm

I began recovering from the terrible experience I believe was purposed to happen from the time I was placed in my mother's womb. We do not know what our lives consist of until the journey of life begins. The wounds were deep and the healing is ongoing. But, I had my life back despite its condition. However, I became suspicious of everyone I encountered. Everyone became a suspect. But, I was raising my children as a single parent and loving every minute.

My focus became my children and building a new life for myself. The thought of starting a new relationship didn't cross my mind. I learned how to survive for me and my children. With the help of welfare, the monthly check was coming in, and I got my children into day care. I needed to know that while I was at work, I could have peace of mind. It was hard to place my children on the little yellow day care bus each morning and watch their tiny faces pressed against the window pane with tears in their eyes. But, I had to work because welfare was not a permanent place for me.

Even though I was surrounded by people, I felt alone. I went through the security process of finger printing and lying when asked if I was pregnant. I needed this job not just for me but for my children. It was just them and me in a world that I perceived as a living hell. After I got the job, they gave me a check to buy what they called a professional wardrobe.

In the 1970's, working in the government, you were not allowed to wear pants. Dresses and skirt suits were the only attire allowed. Now, you can come to work looking like a disco queen and no one will approach you about your attire.

My first government job at grade level GS-2 was just enough to carry me from paycheck to paycheck with the welfare assistance check. When I reported to welfare that I was working full-time, they cut my check. It was crazy, but I did not give in to the system.

There were so many women on welfare back then just because, and they would not attend the educational program so they could get off. They liked staying home and having babies, just so their checks would increase monthly. I had made up my mind this was not for me. And, as soon as my job started promoting me, I got off welfare. It was the happiest day of my life. I remained in the same apartment despite all the bad memories there, because my children and I needed a place to stay and it was not easy to find a decent apartment with three children.

Men started having an interest in me, but my heart was still cold. I had two pursuers sitting in my living room one day, each trying to out-sit the other. I was not interested in either one of them. But, it came time for me to choose between them to remain respectful in the eyes of my children.

These were my choices: Man #1 was in a relationship with someone else who was pregnant at the time, and the other one was going through a divorce. You know, I was not going to get involved with a man who had a woman pregnant and was running after me; he had to go. So, I started dating the one who was going through a divorce. What a man. He was as close to a virgin as you could get.

Man #2 was raised Catholic and refused to sleep with me while he was still married to another woman. Today, I am married to this man and we have been together for 40 years (lived together for five years and legally married for thirty-five years.) I took this man through pure hell because of the scars that had not healed from my seven-year abusive relationship. I know this man was sent by God, because he tolerated my foolishness for the five years we lived together.

By now, I was chasing time trying to fill moments of my life that were gone. You can't go back to the past and expect to pick up where you left off. For five years, I ran from club to club partying until dawn, then went to work without going to sleep. The drugs made it possible for me to do this because now I had graduated to the "rock," and I was at the point of no return. I needed help and had no one to turn to. I would drive home and wake up in my driveway, not knowing how I got there.

One morning, I came home from a night of partying and my husband was waiting for me. He asked for a divorce. I was so drunk that I told him to get a lawyer and I would sign the papers. My mother called and asked if I had lost my mind. She said my husband had called her and shared what was on his heart. I was hurting the man who loved me unconditionally. I was letting my past hurts destroy my marriage. I came to my senses and realized the same pattern that had been operating in our family for years was putting me on the brim of this destruction ready to destroy me and my family.

When I decided to stop running the streets, my husband would not sleep with me and refused to touch me. I was now hurting again, but this time, the pain was instituted by me. I cleaned up my act, but it was as if my husband was punishing me. Finally, he came back to me and, once again, God showed up and saved my marriage. We confessed to each other everything we had done out of anger and disappointment. Today, our marriage is healed and we are as one flesh, the way a husband and wife were created to be from the beginning.

I began experiencing a different type of abuse and it was ruining my family. We were all under the same roof but living apart. My children had started to go to church on Sundays, but this did not faze me. I was caught up in my own hell. I remember my daughters coming home from church one Sunday and asking me if I would attend church with them on Mother's Day.

The desire to go to church was not in me but, to pacify them, I agreed to go. It was an unusual time for me. When I walked through the doors of the church, I remember sitting on the left side of the sanctuary and the pastor giving the mothers phone-calling cards. I never used the calling card and still have it to this day. Church was over and I was happy to go home. My mind was already made up that I would not return to that place called church.

The next Sunday, it was as if I had lost control of my actions and something else had taken over. I found myself in the shower preparing to go back to that place called church. In the next moment, I found myself walking through the doors of the same church I had attended with my daughters for Mother's Day.

The pastor was in the pulpit, and it seemed like I was the only one in the sanctuary when he gave the benediction. I did not plan to respond, but suddenly, found myself moving towards the altar. It felt like I was floating instead of walking. When I arrived at the altar, there appeared to be a white light and I could barely see, but then again, I found myself moving from in front of the altar. I was moving towards another part of the church. I ended up in an upstairs room where people were handing out pamphlets and talking.

When I returned home, I went to the basement and took anything that looked like drugs and flushed them down the toilet. My brother came to visit and asked me for a beer. I told him to take every beer that was in the refrigerator, because during this last visit to church, I received total deliverance from drugs, alcohol, and smoking.

My life had taken a different path and I knew it was all because of the prayers of my children. They were so excited. I remember my children crying and telling people that they had gotten their mother back. What a wonderful experience to receive Jesus Christ as my Lord and Savior and deliverance simultaneously!

The new path I was now on changed the way I talked (no cursing), the way I dressed, and the way I treated my husband and children. Before the salvation, I lived as if no one mattered but me. When I turned my life around, I lost friends and a close relationship with one of my sisters. She and I were like white on rice but, I later learned, it wasn't a real relationship. It was all about something we had in common — drugs. Living your life in the way God intended will make you feel alone. All I did was read the Bible; and no one I had associated with before my deliverance wanted to hear about the Bible. No one called or came to see me. It was a lonely time in my life until I had established my relationship with Jesus.

I rededicated my life to the Lord because He was with me when I was in those dark places of my life. It was God who saved my life more than once. If it had not been for the Lord, my life would have ended many years ago. But, because of my preordained purpose and destiny, I am writing this story. My life is not my own and never was, so who am I to destroy it? How can you destroy something that does not belong to you?

Chapter 10

Happily Married - My Life as a Wife

Trials and tribulations occur in every aspect of life. For the married and single woman, maintaining purity in your covenant relationships is only possible through the divine and intimate relationship you have established with God through Jesus Christ. Matthew 6:33 NKJV says it clearly: "But seek ye first the kingdom of God and His righteousness and all things will be added unto you." I believe God chose me to minister to women on the importance of "Purity in Marriage," not just to married women, but also to single women who are anticipating marriage.

When I became a wife on May 8, 1981, there was no support group of any kind. I was on my own. So, through trial and error, I battled every demon that can possibly be named to maintain my marriage with the word "purity." Let me be transparent, unveiled, naked, and free. We are all women so why not be real? In the beginning, my marriage was a dream come true. But, then came the time when I had to be in charge while my husband worked two jobs.

Satan was obviously at my window peeping in, because he knew my desire was not to be alone. And, he made evil look good and temptation allowable. But God, who knew beyond the flesh, had a purpose and plan for my life that was predestined before the foundations of the world and before I was formed in my mother's womb – Jeremiah 1:5, NKJV. God had already traveled to my end and was satisfied that I could handle the trip to destiny. I am still on that journey. And, none of us have reached the mark. It's an ongoing process.

There is an appointed place and time God has predestined for us. And, He promised that He will never leave us nor forsake us - Hebrews 13:5, KJV. He is closer than a brother. This all sounds good now, but you know, in the beginning it was a struggle to get the way we are today; and some of us are still struggling. But, God can make what seems impossible possible according to:

Matthew 19:26, NKJV - "With man this is impossible but with God all things are possible."

The flesh still wants to have its way. The flesh always wants to be right. The flesh wants to be the first and last, but nobody and nothing can take the throne of our God. He is Alpha and Omega, the beginning, and the end, the first and the last. We all have been tempted, are being tempted, and will be tempted, but God has equipped us and given each of us a way out.

We are experiencing spiritual warfare. Married women, God is holding us responsible to keep our marriages holy and pure. We are to honor our husbands regardless of how we feel. It's not about our feelings or emotions. It's about keeping the commandments God has given us concerning our marriages. Abstaining from sex because of our attitudes is sinful and opens the door for the enemy to come in and destroy our families and our marriages.

Deliverance and healing will bring us out of the valley of dead bones. Fasting and praying to keep from having sex is a sin when it's done in a derogatory way. This can only take place when both parties have agreed and consented.

Today's society has "drifted" from God's idea of purity in marriage. In our world, we are bombarded with adulterous themes from movies and television shows, reports of infidelity by athletes, movie stars, and politicians, and the proliferation of internet pornography. To the casual observer, it might seem as if the world accepts and condones sexual immorality and adultery. Fortunately, we have God's Word as an anchor point to show how far we have drifted from His idea. In one key passage, Solomon discusses the topic of adultery.

Most people are fully aware that adultery is explicitly spelled out as a sin in the Ten Commandments, yet it continues to be a problem in our society, just as it was in Solomon's day. Even some self-professed "Christians" are committing adultery at an alarming rate, as more and more people find ways to rationalize their sinful behavior. They wrongly believe that God might condone their behavior or give them a "free pass" if they spend one hour a week sitting in church and the rest of the time cheating on their spouses.

God, however, makes it perfectly clear throughout the Bible that adultery is the opposite of His plan for our marriages. In one verse, Solomon warns that, "the lips of an adulteress drip honey, and her speech is smoother than oil; but in the end, she is bitter as gall, sharp as a double-edged sword. Her feet go down to death; her steps lead straight to the grave" – Proverbs 5: 3-5, NKJV. In addition, our Lord and Savior Jesus Christ said, "I tell you that anyone who looks at a woman lustfully has already committed adultery with her in his heart" - Matthew 5:28, NKJV.

For the modern Christian, adultery means a lot more than just infidelity. What some people fail to realize is that the wandering eye, flirting, and pornography are just as damaging to the marriage relationship as cheating; and are, therefore, completely against God's will for us.

So, what is God's ideal for marriage? To answer that, let us first remember that God is the one who designed marriage in the first place. Marriage was not an idea that began through any government; it came directly from God. He designed marriage as a covenantal relationship between a man and woman, and expects it to be kept pure and holy.

The truth is that your spouse is a divine gift from God and should be treated as such. Instead of looking for other ways to fulfill desires based on the illusion of greener pastures, God wants us to find pleasure and happiness in the relationship He gave us. Solomon reminds us to, "Drink water from your own cistern, running water from your own well" – Proverbs 5:15, NKJV. Purity in marriage is vital in building a healthy and lasting relationship.

Regardless of what the world believes, there is no substitute for complete and total purity when it comes to your spouse. It is up to each of us, as followers of Christ, to guarantee our spouses this level of purity, as we always remember that, "a man's ways are in full view of the LORD" – Proverbs 5:21, NKJV. Do not settle for anything less than God's absolute best for your marriage.

God will not save you. Why? Because He does not want us to seek Him in a way that denies the very body that He gave us—a body with needs to be met and desires to be fulfilled. The same is true for us regarding sex. If you seek to pursue Christlikeness through a year-long intimacy fast, do not expect Jesus to shield you from all the trappings of our sex-crazed culture. Paul has negative things to say to those who seek to pursue a righteousness that denies their own earthiness:

Colossians 2:21-23

1 Timothy 4:1-5

To seek celibacy as a way of life, as a married man or woman, is dangerous. And the reason Paul commands married couples to decide upon these things mutually is because one partner may have a sex drive that is not even half as intense as their spouse's. Your job as a husband or wife is not to force your own gifts or abilities on your spouse, as if he or she should get up to speed with your superior Christlikeness, but to serve your spouse as a servant of Jesus Christ as a fellow, dependent creature. No two people will have the same sex drive.

God offers the Christian two options: either no marriage and no sex or marriage and a lot of sex (or at least enough to keep yourself and your spouse from temptation). This is how the Christian glorifies God in His body. The unmarried are not to have even a little sex, and the married are permitted to abstain from sexual intercourse for only one purpose: to devote themselves to prayer and fasting, but this decision must be mutually agreed upon and must only be for a short period of time.

Paul's clear teaching is that it is better for a married couple to err on the side of having too much sex rather than having too little sex. If you are married, you must not simply seek to fulfill your spouse's needs, but to do so with conviction. Jesus does not just permit sex in marriage; He commands it in marriage. Jesus, however, does not permit prolonged or frequent celibacy in marriage. Thus, the way to pursue purity in the context of marriage is through having sex. The Christian is to run from sexual immorality. But, one of the primary ways a married man or woman runs from sexual immorality is by running to sexual fulfillment in marriage.

Chapter 11

Grandmother – Going Back to School

In 1975, I became a white-collar worker, although my education was limited after dropping out of school in the ninth grade. While on welfare, I enrolled in a school to learn and equip myself with the basics (i.e. typing, writing, English). Now, the day has come to take the OPM test that will determine what entry level I qualify for. Entering the government at the GS-2 level just got my foot in the door.

My first supervisor presented the chance to obtain my GED. This was a wonderful opportunity to move me to the next level and take me out of the clerical position into data processing, as an edit analyst. Working in a data processing office, there are many opportunities for advancement. As a black female in the white-collar world back in the early 70's, one was required to have a backbone.

Promotions came few and far between, but not without consistency and persistency in what I believed. Sleeping with management was not an option. I declared my children would not have to experience what I did while pursuing their education and establishing their careers.

First, my working with a senior developer (white) and being a strong-willed black woman did not mix well in the government and gave all the warning signs of trouble in the camp. One day, while debating an issue and believing that I was right, the situation escalated into a difference of opinion battle until finally he said, "You are a spicy wench!" Having dignity, it was easy for me to ignore his response knowing that I won the battle.

This time of my life would prove to be a good lesson to later share with my children, as to not planting bad seeds about other ethnic groups and to educate them on what opportunities existed. But they would have to believe in themselves and ignore those who are ignorant to their existence. I was determined to keep my job and have the same equal opportunities available to me that my forefathers fought and died for. I was not going to disappoint them.

Abraham Lincoln wrote The Emancipation Proclamation, meaning that we all have equal rights despite our skin color. A quote from Abraham Lincoln's collection of work is: "I want every man to have the chance - and I believe a black man is entitled to it - in which he can better his condition, when he may look forward and hope to be a hired laborer this year and the next, work for himself afterward, and finally to hire men to work for him. That is the true system." (http://www.alincoln-library.com/abraham-lincoln-quotes.shtml)

The year 2007 proved a time to focus on further enhancing my life, since my children were grown and no longer required my undivided attention. I had so much free time and needed to put it to good use. So, I decided to focus on my dream of going back to school and obtaining a college degree, not knowing how far I would go.

One day, while listening to the radio, I heard a man celebrating his achievement of obtaining his master's degree. This man was 80 years old and inspired me so much that I immediately shared this information with my husband. We agreed that now was the time for me to pursue my dreams by going back to school. I had no idea I would accomplish so much. Within seven years, I obtained three degrees: An Associate of Arts, a Bachelor of Science, and a Master's degree. Working full-time, being a wife, mother, grandmother, an ordained licensed minister and attending online classes was challenging, but doable. The most challenging part of all was maintaining a balanced life.

There were times when the road became tough and I couldn't see the light at the end of the tunnel. This required spiritual encouragement and believing what the Word of God says: (I quoted it every day): "I can do all things through Christ who strengthens me" - Philippians 4:13, NKJV. My colleagues were asking questions such as: How can you do what you do and still come to work and perform with excellence? This opened the door for me to share God's grace and mercy (because without Him none of this would have been possible). I would respond, "Only God is keeping and sustaining me, so that I can complete this educational journey."

During this journey, the spirit of the Lord inspired me to start a Bible Study group for three years. I used the material from the book "Purpose Driven Life." In this class were managers, other workers in the building, as well as colleagues. What an experience. When that season ended, I knew in my heart that God was preparing me for higher dimensions in Him.

Chapter 12

A Mother's Love – Her Children

Joy and inheritance sums up the love between a mother and her daughters. Daughters are like precious stones. Each stone is shaped and buffed into perfection. The relationship-building is initiated from inception within the womb. Each child is uniquely designed by God's blueprint. No two children are alike. I truly believe, for each child, that a parent has already been given what is needed to nurture that child into the person God has predestined and preordained each child to become — who He has called them to be.

A mother's love cannot be measured but can only be experienced through the bonding relationship between a mother and child which started in the womb. Reality sets in when you feel that first kick. You watch the movements of your stomach and suddenly, an impression of a knee appears.

The knot begins to move across your belly and you get excited because this is your first experience as a pregnant woman. Another special moment is when you are alone, it's quiet, and suddenly, you think you hear this sucking sound, realizing it's the baby inside the cavity of your stomach sucking her thumb.

You think to yourself; this is truly amazing. Although, your baby is still in the womb, your baby can move, make sounds, and even hear what's going on outside. The time is drawing near for you to bring this precious gift from God into the world. You have been preparing for this special day for nine months. It's a girl. Oh, what a happy time! Your girl baby is here, and you have been given a special responsibility to nurture and love this little creature.

A Letter to My Oldest Daughter on Her Engagement

My dearest, I have watched you grow from when you were trying to do everything in your power to keep from coming into this world, then growing into a little girl who I didn't think was going to be potty trained so you could stay at day care.

You did not want me to leave you. I remember watching the little yellow bus as it drove away with your tiny face pressed against the window and you were crying. I cried as I left the small apartment we lived in and climbed the hill on a hot sunny day to catch the bus [laugh].

As you grew a little more into a grade-school child, I swore you were going to be a hair stylist someday because of the rather interesting styles you would come up with. One or two ponytails were not enough. Sometimes it had to be three or four and all in different directions, sometimes all on one side and sometimes all on top. It did not matter, as long as it was as many as you wanted, where you wanted them. I will not ever forget the many times I would sit and put your hair in little tiny braids all over your head with many colorful barrettes.

Then, you grew a little more and started to make friends for the first time. First, there was your best friend who lived around the corner and down the street from our house. And, I will never forget the friend that lived up the street. You girls were tight and inseparable and they are here with you today, to share in your special day, like many days in the past, regardless of the distance between you. They have ended up being your lifetime best friends and I know you will keep each other close in your hearts and your minds forever. There were even more girlfriends, but I cannot remember them all. Two of your best friends who lived closest to you were your running partners. I remember insisting that you and your girlfriend go and look for your sister. It's funny now, but it wasn't then. There are so many memories I could share but I won't. These are the memories I will keep in my heart forever.

As you grew, the men started coming into your life. Men other than your father and brothers. There was your first crush, who you said you were always going to marry when you grew up, and who ended up breaking your heart. Then, came the love of your life. You were like two peas in a pod. The two of you went through many of life's storms not knowing that God had already blessed and predestined your wedding day.

Now comes the part of this letter, which will be the hardest for me. Just like your dad, who will walk you down the aisle and give you away, I too, must give you away, in a sense. There are so many things I have tried to teach you, protect you from, and show you how to do. I could not possibly list them all.

The one thing I have never tried to protect you from is love. Love of family, friends, and now, the love you share with your husband-to-be. I could not be happier for you. I do wish you both the best you could ever possibly have and hope for. Love each other unconditionally, never go to bed angry, and never say "it wasn't my fault." Marriage is a contract between two people through thick and thin. Whether it's high waters or no waters, you are in this partnership for a life time.

Always be the virtuous woman and soon-to-be wife that God created you to be. Behind every good man is a strong and supportive woman. You are the pillar in this relationship and will be the strength of your household. Remember, I am here for you always, but there is one that you should always seek first   God Himself. May you exceed the years of marriage your father and I have had so far. Let this marriage be a witness to those who will follow.

Love You Always,

Mommie

A Letter to My Youngest Daughter at Her Engagement

To My Dear Daughter,

How do I love you in so many ways? As your mother, it's difficult to describe the love, laughter, and life you have brought into my life. There are so many memories I have kept locked up in a secret place where I go to from time to time. You were such a beautiful baby with a head full of curly locks and a face with a glowing, almond pigmentation. You were always standing in your crib looking over at me before I noticed you were ready to start your day.

As you grew from an infant to a toddler, at the age of 4, everyone wanted you to be their little girl. Especially Aunt Theresa, who wanted to take you home with her and raise you as her own. She would come and get you on weekends. But your dad had captured your heart. I remember how you would run out of the house with nothing on but your undies because you thought your daddy would leave you. And, no one could ride in the front seat of the car but you.

When your brother was born (Leon III), the jealousy was so obvious we had to gently try and make you understand that nothing had changed in the relationship between you and your daddy. It was so funny to watch how you and your brother would scramble trying to outrun each other to see who would get to the car first and claim the front seat. Now, moving into the memories of your teen years, we would battle over my position when it came to who set the rules as it related to what time you should be home. There were many nights I would sit up all night long waiting for you to come home. This was the case with all your siblings. But you were a hard case. One thing for sure, I never stopped waiting on my baby girl to come home.

As I look back over the years to see how you have grown into such a beautiful woman of God, I realize that it was worth every moment, every tear, and all the laughter we have shared together. There was a specific time in our relationship where we had grown apart and it hurt. For years, I would pray and ask God to please mend our relationship as mother and daughter. I realized that I caused the strain and stress on our relationship because I was not there when you really needed me. My presence was there but it was not as a mom, but someone passing through.

Oh, how blind I was. I missed those years that I wasted not being the mother that I should have been, but we serve an awesome God Who sustains us even though we ignore Him. You taught me how to listen, instead of always giving my opinion, when all you really wanted was someone to hear with their heart and ears. You are an awesome daughter.

There came a time when healing took place and we were reunited as mother and daughter through the power and might of God Himself. Sitting in my bedroom floor, we shared a moment I will never forget. The hurt and pain bottled up in both of us burst forth in such a way that we knew God was present through our reconciliation. I love you more now than ever. You have grown into a beautiful woman, mother, and soon-to-be wife. Now, the time has come for me to release you into the arms of your husband. I have held you closer than ever. It's not easy letting you go to start your new life and journey; but, I promise I will always be here for you, as your mom and friend.

Love You Always,
Mommie

Chapter 13

Personal Prayers and Declarations

You must pray for those around you. Is there no one who doesn't need your prayers? How many colleagues do you have? How many neighbors do you have? How many relatives and friends do you have? Always ask the Lord to place one or two special persons in your heart. When the Lord places a person in your heart, He intends to save this person through you. You should write down his name in your record book and continually bring him to the Lord through prayer.

You need to set aside a fixed time each day for this work of intercession. Whether it be an hour, half an hour, or a quarter of an hour, it must be a fixed time. If there is no fixed time for prayer, there will not be definite prayer. As a result, there will not be any prayer at all. Hence, always fix a time for prayers, whether it is a quarter of an hour or half an hour.

Do not be too ambitious; do not plan for two hours and end up not being able to carry it out. It is more practical to set aside one hour, half an hour, or a quarter of an hour. Always fix a time to pray for those who need your prayer. Do not relax. Do this every day. After a while, you will see sinners saved one by one.

A Prayer and Declaration for Healing

Father, in the Name of Jesus, I confess Your Word concerning health and healing. As I do, I believe that Your Word will not return to You void, but it will accomplish what it says. In the Name of Jesus, I believe that I am healed according to 1 Peter 2:24, NKJV. Your Word says that Jesus Himself took my infirmities and bore my sicknesses - Matthew 8:17 NKJV; therefore, with great boldness and confidence, I stand on the authority of Your Word and declare that I am redeemed from the curse of sickness. I refuse to tolerate its symptoms.

Satan, I speak to you in Jesus's Name and I proclaim that your principalities, powers, rulers of the darkness of this world, and spiritual wickedness in heavenly places are bound from operating against me in any way. I am loosed from your assignment. I am the property of Almighty God and I give you no place in me. I dwell in the secret place of the Most High God and I abide under the shadow of the Almighty, whose power no foe can withstand.

Now, Father, I believe Your Word says that the angel of the Lord encamps round about me and delivers me from every evil work. No evil shall befall me, no plague or calamity shall come near my dwelling – Psalm 91, NKJV.

I confess that the Word abides in me and it is life and medicine to my flesh. The law of the Spirit of life in Christ Jesus operates in me, making me free from the law of sin and death. I hold fast to my confession of Your Word and I stand immovable, knowing that health and healing are mine now, in Jesus Name. Amen.

A Prayer for Healing

Father, in the name of Jesus, I come before You, asking You to heal me. It is written that the prayer of faith will save the sick, and the Lord will raise him up. And, if I have committed sins, I will be forgiven. I let go of all unforgiveness, resentment, anger and bad feelings toward anyone.

My body is the temple of the Holy Spirit, and I desire to be in good health. I seek truth that will make me free – both spiritual and natural (good eating habits, medications if necessary, and appropriate rest and exercise). You bought me at a price, and I desire to glorify you in my spirit and my body – they both belong to you.

Thank you, Father, for sending your Word to heal me and deliver me from all my destructions. Jesus, You are the Word who became flesh and dwelt among us. You bore my griefs (pains) and carried my sorrows (sickness). You were pierced through for my transgressions, crushed for my iniquities; the chastening for my well-being fell upon You, and by your scourging I am healed.

Father, I give attention to your words, and incline my ear to your sayings. I will not let them depart from my sight, but keep them in my heart. For they are my life and health to my whole body.

Since the Spirit of Him who raised Jesus from the dead dwells in me, He who raised Christ from the dead will also give life to my mortal body through His Spirit who dwells in me. Thank You that I will prosper and be in health even as my soul prospers. Amen.

Prayer of An Intercessor

Father, I know that You have called me as an Intercessor and I intercede on behalf of the Metropolitan Area (Maryland, District of Columbia, and Virginia). Lord, I am at your disposal. I am honored that You have chosen me to go and minister your Word and your Life. Because You have called me, whatever I set my hand to will prosper and you will accompany me with signs and wonders. I am Your Ambassador and I will represent You well.

I am willing and committed to the call. I avail myself to You. Your harvest is waiting for the Laborers to bring in the bounty, so You and only You get the glory and honor. Lord, I pray this assignment is a divine manifestation by You to begin Bible Study in the Metropolitan Area. Lord, help me to crucify my flesh daily with the Word. In Jesus' Powerful Name. Amen!

A Prayer of Personal Declarations

I declare and decree that you are blessed of the Lord.

I declare and decree you have favor with God and man.

I declare and decree wealth and riches are in your house.

I declare and decree you are a virtuous woman of God.

I declare and decree no weapon formed against you shall prosper.

God will make your enemies your footstool. I decree an open heaven over you and your family.

I release the angels of the Lord to guard and protect you. I release the blood of Jesus upon you.

I command the blessings of the Lord to chase after you and overtake you.

I declare and decree strength and honor are your clothing. You will rejoice in time to come. When you open your mouth, wisdom flows and your tongue is the law of kindness. You watch over the ways of your household and the bread of idleness you do not partake of. Your husband calls you blessed and praises you. You and your husband are king and queen in your kingdom. Your beauty and charm are apparent, but because you fear the Lord you will be praised. You are your husband's help-mate. I declare and decree you will receive the fruit of your hands and your own works will praise you in the Kingdom.

I release your helpers from the east, west, north, and south. God is raising up women of integrity and character to be your handmaidens. Do not be dismayed; for those who wait on the Lord, their strength shall be renewed. I pray that those who do not have your best interest at heart will be exposed, revealed, and removed. The Lord will place women of God around and about you who do have your best interest at heart, who will be your eyes and ears to serve you the way God intended, in Jesus' name. Amen.

Declaring Psalm 22

Psalm 22:3 says, "God inhabits the praises of His people." Our praise brings God personally on the scene. At times of high praise, the shekinah glory of God will fill an entire place with His sweet presence.

When Solomon finished building the house of the Lord, the trumpeters and singers lifted their voices as one, and with trumpets, cymbals, and instruments of music, they praised the Lord saying, "For he is good; for his mercy endureth forever." The glory of God filled the house so that the priests could not even minister because of the cloud (2 Chronicles 5:13-14, NKJV). God Himself inhabited the praises of His people.

So, usher His presence into your situation. Praise Him during your needs. Praise Him, regardless of your feelings. Obey the Word and praise Him continually. He is worthy to be praised! To praise when you don't feel like it is an act of honor.

Scripture Reading: Revelation 5:7-10

I decree and declare, today is the day of high expectations and the dawn of new possibilities, "Therefore glorify the LORD in the dawning light" (Isaiah 24:15, NKJV).

Every new day with God brings the dawn of new and better possibilities. Today could turn out to be the best day of your life, but how it ends largely depends on how you begin it. You can take control of your day from its very beginning—as you command your morning, and as you do, know whatever begins with God will end right. No matter how good or bad your life is, every circumstance can change for the best if you learn how to command your morning before your day begins.

Father, I stand and declare today is a new day. Every element of my day shall cooperate with Your purpose and destiny for me. Anything or anyone assigned to undermine, frustrate, hinder, or hurt me, I command to be moved out of my sphere of influence.

Lord, bless the works of my hands. Let my name be associated with good things. Shield me from persecution and false accusations; guard me against greed, discouragement, and sabotage. I welcome opportunities to grow and mature. Let my actions be in sync with Your will, in Jesus' name. Amen.

Praying the Prayer of a Virtuous Woman on Behalf of My Husband

---

Father, in the name of Jesus, I take Your Word and speak it out of my mouth and say that I have faith that I am a capable, intelligent, patient, and a virtuous woman. I am far more precious than jewels. My value to my husband and family is far above rubies and pearls.

The heart of my husband trusts me confidently and relies on and believes in me completely, so that he has no lack of honest gain or need of dishonest spoil.

Father, I will comfort, encourage, and do him only good while there is life within me. I gird myself with strength and spiritual, mental, and physical fitness for my God-given task. I taste and see that my gain from work with and for God is good. My lamp does not go out; it burns continually through the night of any trouble, privation, or sorrow, and it warns away fear, doubt, and distrust.

I open my hand to the poor. I reach out my filled hands to the needy – whether in spirit, soul, or body. My husband is known as a success in everything he puts his hand to. Strength and dignity are my clothing, and my position in my household is strong. I am secure and at peace in knowing that my family is in a position of readiness for the future.

I open my mouth with skillful and Godly wisdom, and in my tongue is the law of kindness and love. I look well to how things go in my household. The bread of idleness, gossip, discontent, and self-pity I will not eat.

My children, rise up and call me blessed and happy. My husband boasts and praises me, saying that I excel in all I set my hand to. I am a woman who reverently and sincerely loves You, Lord, and You shall give me the fruits of my hands. My works will praise me wherever I go, for Father, I confess that I am a submitted wife – simply because I want to be and I recognize Your authority. I thank You for my husband who is over me, but who has given me (through the chain of command) the necessary power to do what Your Word says for me to do from Proverbs 31:10-31, NKJV. I am as this woman is – a loving, successful, submitted wife – in the name of Jesus. Amen.

Praying and Interceding for My Pastors/Ministers

Father, in the name of Jesus, I pray and confess that the Spirit of the Lord shall rest upon Bishop Kibby ...the spirit of wisdom and understanding, the spirit of counsel and might, the spirit of knowledge. I pray that as Your Spirit rests upon Bishop Kibby, He will make him of quick understanding because You, Lord, have anointed and qualified him to preach the Gospel to the meek, the poor, the wealthy, the afflicted. You have sent Bishop Kibby to bind up and heal the broken-hearted, to proclaim liberty to the physical and spiritual captives, and to proclaim the opening of the prison and of the eyes to those who are bound.

My Pastor shall be called the priest of the Lord. People will speak of him as a minister of God. He shall eat the wealth of nations. I pray and believe no weapon that is formed against him shall prosper and any tongue that rises against him in judgment shall be shown to be in the wrong.

I pray that You prosper him abundantly, Lord – physically, spiritually, and financially.

I confess he holds fast and follows the pattern of wholesome and sound teaching in all faith and love which is for us in Christ Jesus. He guards and keeps with the greatest love the precious and excellently adapted Truth which has been entrusted to him by the Holy Spirit who makes His home in him.

Lord, I pray and believe every day freedom of utterance is given him, that he will open his mouth boldly and courageously, as he ought to do to get the Gospel to the people. Thank you, Lord, for the added strength which comes superhumanly that You have given him.

I hereby confess that I shall stand behind my Pastor and undergird him in prayer. I will say only that good thing that will edify him. I will not allow myself to judge him, but will continue to intercede for him and speak and pray blessings upon him in the name of Jesus. Thank You, Jesus, for the answers. Hallelujah! Amen.

Scriptures

Isaiah 11:2,3; Isaiah 61:1,6; Isaiah 54:17; 2 Timothy 1:13,14; Ephesians 6:19,20; 1 Peter 3:12

Incredible Prayer of a Praying Woman

Father, in the name of Jesus, I demand, command, and decree your (the reader's) release from every yoke, bondage, imprisonment, and every soul tie. I command you to be untied from that which has you bound through the witness of the blood of Christ. I declare your soul is the Lord's. I command the chains around your hands, feet, and neck to be broken. I command walls of confinement to fall. I command you to leap over walls that have resisted you all these years. May you run through every troop; and in the name of Jesus I confer upon you fresh oil, fresh power, supernatural power of deliverance, and new beginnings.

I confer upon you that miracle of divine protection, deliverance, provision, and favor. I command a new stirring of God within your spirit man. I command you to rise up and take hold of God as never before. I reinstate your prayer life and spiritual sensitivity. Before Heaven and Earth, I declare that nothing will take your place.

Now, lift your hands and pray this prayer with me:

Satan, take your hands off my life, my husband, my children, my home, my church, and my community. Take your hands off my inheritance, my finances, my health, my progress, my focus, and my prayer life. In Jesus' name, hands off! I will never be the same again. I will not be denied. I will see victory. I will see the salvation of my God in Jesus' mighty name. Amen.

Prodigal Daughter's Declaration (Healing and Wholeness)

I decree and declare the assurance of Your Word that the angel of the Lord encamps around about me and delivers me from every evil work. No evil shall befall me, no plague or calamity shall come near my dwelling.

I decree and declare according to 1 Peter 2:24 – NKJV: "I am healed, in the name of Jesus."

I decree that Your Word will not return to You void, but will accomplish what it says it will: Isaiah 55:1 - NKJV.

I decree on the authority of the written Word that I am redeemed from the curse of sickness and I refuse to tolerate its symptoms.

I confess the Word of God abides in me and delivers me perfect soundness of mind and wholeness in body and spirit from the deepest parts of my nature in my immortal spirit even to the joints and marrow of my bones - Hebrews 4:12, NKJV.

I declare the Word is medication and life to my flesh, for the law of the Spirit of life operates in me and makes me free from the law of sin and death.

I decree the assurance of Your Word that the angel of the Lord encamps around about me and delivers me from every evil work. No evil shall befall me, no plague or calamity shall come near my dwelling - Psalm 91, NKJV.

I decree and declare Your word according to Isaiah 54:17-NKJV: "No weapon formed against me shall prosper and every tongue risen against me I shall condemn. This is the heritage of the saints of the Lord, saith the Lord."

Spiritual Healing and Wholeness

God has given us authority over disease, demons, sickness, and storms. He calls us to establish His authority by our action with divinely empowered speech or words. Then, we may declare that authority in Jesus' name. We can command a storm to be stilled; we can command a demon to come out; we can command affliction to leave; and we can command sickness to depart. To obtain the blessings that God has given to us, we must put action to the spoken Word. Nothing is impossible with God when you have the faith the size of a mustard seed.

Exodus 15:26 - NKJV

And it is said, "If you diligently heed the voice of the Lord your God and do what is right in His sight, give ear to His commandments and keep all His statutes, I will put none of the diseases on you which I have brought on the Egyptians. For I am the Lord who heals (Jehovah Raphe) you."

I declare and decree that sickness and disease cannot operate in my body. I take authority and command sickness to leave my body now in Jesus' name.

Deuteronomy 7:15 - NKJV

And the Lord will take away from thee all sickness, and will put none of the evil diseases of Egypt, which thou knowest, upon thee, but will lay them upon all them, that hate thee.

I command all sicknesses and evil diseases to go back to the sender in Jesus' name. Let any sickness rooted in my body be plucked up in Jesus' name.

Psalm 107:20 - NKJV

He sent His Word, and healed them, and delivered them from their destructions.

I decree and declare the Lord sent His Word and delivered me from any destruction. I am redeemed from destruction.

Psalm 103:2,3 - NKJV
Bless the Lord, O my soul, and forget not all His benefits: Who forgiveth all thine iniquities; Who healeth all thy diseases.

Lord, I declare and decree, "You healed all of my diseases," in Jesus' name.

Isaiah 33:24 - NKJV
And the inhabitant shall not say, I am sick: the people that dwell therein shall be forgiven their iniquity.

I declare and decree the enemy shall not spoil me, but he will be spoiled in Jesus' name.

Jeremy 7:14 - NKJV
Heal me, O Lord, and I shall be healed; save me, and I shall be saved: for thou art my praise. Let every yoke of sickness be destroyed in Jesus' name.

Psalm 118:17 - NKJV
I shall not die, but live, and declare the works of the Lord.

I prophesy to every dry bone in my life and command it to live in Jesus' name.

Matthew 9:6 - NKJV

But that ye may know that the Son of man hath power on earth to forgive sins, (then saith He to the sick of the palsy), Arise, take up thy bed, and go unto thine house.

Matthew 8:16,17 – NKJV

When the even was come, they brought unto Him many that were possessed with devils: and He cast out the spirits with His word, and healed all who were sick.

That it might be fulfilled which was spoken by Esaias the prophet, saying, Himself too, our infirmities and bare our sicknesses.

Jesus carried my sickness and infirmities. I cast out all spirits of infirmity that would attack my body in Jesus' name. I break and rebuke all curses of sickness and infirmity in Jesus' name.

1 Peter 2:24 – NKJV

Who His own self bares our sins in His own body on the tree, that we, being dead to sins, should live unto righteousness: by whose stripes ye were healed.

Isaiah 53:5 - NKJV

But He was wounded for our transgressions; He was bruised for our iniquities: the chastisement of our peace was upon Him; and with His stripes we are healed.

I am healed by the stripes of Jesus, in Jesus' name.

Psalms 30: 2, 3 - NKJV

2 O Lord my God, I cried unto thee, and thou hast healed me.

3 O Lord, thou hast brought up my soul from the grave: thou hast kept me alive, that I should not go down to the pit.

Spiritual Wholeness

Luke 8: 48

The woman with the issue of blood touches the hem of Jesus' garment, and Jesus said to her: "Daughter, be of good cheer; your faith has made you well (whole). Go in peace."

I declare and decree my faith has made me whole, in Jesus Name. Amen.

Luke 8:50 - NKJV

The little girl that was restored to life was by the authority of the spoken Word: "After being told the little girl is dead: Jesus declares: "Only believe, and she will be made well (whole)."

I declare and decree that my belief has made me well, in Jesus Name. Amen.

Mark 10:51,52 - NKJV

Blind Bartimaeus

51 So Jesus answered and said to him, "What do you want Me to do for you?" The blind man said to Him, "Rabboni, that I may receive my sight."
52 Then Jesus said to him, "Go your way; your faith has made you well (whole)." And immediately he received his sight and followed Jesus on the road.

I declare and decree because of my faith I am no longer blind but I can now see, in Jesus' name. Amen.

Confessions and Declarations Using Bible Scriptures

I declare that no weapon formed against me shall prosper, and every tongue which rises against me in judgment I shall condemn. This is the heritage of the servants of the Lord, and their righteousness is from Me, says the Lord. (Isaiah 54:17)

I cast down vain imaginations and every high thing that exalteth itself against the knowledge of God, and I bring every thought captive to the obedience of the Lord Jesus Christ. (2 Corinthians 10:5)

I have been reconciled to Christ, qualified to share in His in heritance, firmly rooted, grounded, built up, established in my faith, and overflowing with thanksgiving.
(2 Corinthians 5:18; Colossians 1:12; Colossians 2:7)

 I tread upon serpents and scorpions and over all the power of the enemy. I take my shield of faith and quench every fiery dart of the enemy. Greater is He Who is in me than he who is in the world. (Psalm 91:13, Ephesians 6:16, 1 John 4:4)

I am a world overcomer because I am born of God. I represent the Father and Jesus well. I am a useful member in the Body of Christ. I am His workmanship recreated in Christ Jesus. My Father God is all the while effectually at work in me both to will and do His good pleasure. (1 John 5:4-5, Ephesians 2:10, Philippians 2:13)

I am a believer and not a doubter. I hold fast to my confession of faith. I decide to walk by faith and practice faith. My faith comes by hearing and hearing by the Word of God. Jesus is the author and finisher of my faith.
(Hebrews 4:14, Hebrews 11:6, Romans 10:17, Hebrews 12:2)

I have the mind of Christ and hold the thoughts, feelings, and purposes of His heart.
(1 Corinthians 2:16)

The Lord is my shepherd. I do not want. My God supplies all my need according to His riches in glory in Christ Jesus.
(Psalm 23:1, Philippians 4:19)

Jesus has been made unto me wisdom, righteousness, sanctification, and redemption. I can do all things through Christ Who strengthens me.

(1 Corinthians 1:30, Philippians 4:13)

Jesus is Lord over my spirit, my soul, and my body. (Philippians 2:9-11)

I declare death and life is in the power of my tongue. And those who love it will eat its fruit. (Proverbs 18:21)

About the Author

Minister Carrie L. Thomas is a native of Denmark, South Carolina. Carrie has dedicated her life to identifying her true self. For 37 years, she has been the proud and happy wife of her best friend and husband Leon C. Thomas, Jr. She is also blessed to have four amazing children: Kelly Wilson-Anderson, Kevin Wilson, Keisha Dyke, and Leon C. Thomas III, as well as four wonderful grandchildren.

Carrie is a graduate of the University of Phoenix, where she received her Associates of Arts in Information Technology Networking, Bachelor of Science in Information Technology, and Master of Information Systems.

After completing her training at Spirit of Faith Bible Institute (SOFBI), Carrie was licensed in 2008 to the Office of Minister, under the tutelage of Drs. Michael A. Freeman and Deloris R. Freeman, at Spirit of Faith Christian Center, in Brandywine, Maryland.

As Vice-President of Community Sisters in Prayer Ministry, Carrie served in the ministry under the guidance of the founder and President, Minister Ruthena Dorsey.

Today, Carrie is the proud founder of Mary Elizabeth's Ministry for the Homeless, in Clinton, Maryland

To the Reader

Some of you may be wondering why I'm writing this book. As a woman, I've carried the hardships, tragedies, and terrifying times from childhood that were buried deep in my subconscious. They were buried because they were too hurtful, or I just didn't want to remember them. I believe my total deliverance and healing will come to pass from writing this book.

The curse stops here. I have confessed my sins, gone through deliverance, and rededicated my life to God. He is the only one who can save us from this corrupt world. If there is any hardness of hearts in the family, we must come together and forgive one another. I'm not just writing a book; this is a letter of how my life went through fire and water and how I survived.

The only way this was possible was nothing more than fulfilling the purpose God predestined for me before I was placed in my mother's womb - Jeremiah 1:5, NKJV. He foreknew me and chose my parents' DNA, but the life I lived then and now was God's plan for using me for such a task as this.

So many people kept telling me, "There is a book on the inside of you that must be written." Ten years ago, I would have never put on paper what I have written here. At this point in my life, I'm not concerned about what you think of me or how you feel about the things I have written. My deepest, heartfelt concern is that someone is set free after they read through the pages of this book. Everything I have written may not apply directly to you, but indirectly, you know somebody, somewhere, who can relate to one of these chapters.

Made in the USA
Middletown, DE
14 September 2021

48298676R00068